Also by Alan C. Greenberg

MEMOS FROM THE CHAIRMAN